The Story of
Facebook

Adam Sutherland

rosen publishing's
rosen
central®

New York

Published in 2012 by The Rosen Publishing Group, Inc.
29 East 21st Street, New York, NY 10010

Commissioning editor: Camilla Lloyd
Designer: Emma Randall
Picture researcher: Shelley Noronha

Library of Congress Cataloging-in-Publication Data

Sutherland, Adam.

 The story of Facebook/Adam Sutherland.
     p. cm.—(The business of high tech)
 Includes bibliographical references and index.
 ISBN 978-1-4488-7042-4 (library binding)—
 ISBN 978-1-4488-7094-3 (pbk.)—
 ISBN 978-1-4488-7095-0 (6-pack)
 1. Facebook (Firm)—History. 2. Facebook (Electronic resource) 3. Online social networks. 4. Zuckerberg, Mark, 1984- 5. Computer software developers—United States. I. Title.
 HM743.F33S88 2012
  006.7'54—dc23
                                                                                    2011037071

Manufactured in the United States of America

CPSIA Compliance Information: Batch #W12YA: For further information, contact Rosen Publishing, New York, New York, at 1-800-237-9932.

Picture Acknowledgments: The author and publisher would like to thank the following for allowing their pictures to be reproduced in this publication: Cover and p. 38: CJG–Technology/Alamy; p. 1 Alex Slobodkin/Istock; throughout background: RedShineStudio/Istock; pp. 4–5, 8–9 © 2003 The Harvard Crimson, Inc. All rights reserved. Reproduced with permission; p. 7 Topfoto/Columbia Pictures; p. 8 Washington Post/Getty Images; pp. 10, 22–23, 34 Bloomberg via Getty Images; pp. 14–15 Adam Sutherland; pp. 12–13 Bloomberg via Getty Images Ramin; p. 11, 20, 32–33, 35, 37 Topfoto; p. 16 Ramin Talaie/Corbis; p. 17 N Nehring/Istock; pp. 18–19 AF Archive/Alamy; p. 26 AP/Press Association; pp. 30–31 Kim Kulish/Corbis CJG; p. 34 Mike Kepka/San Francisco Chronicle/Corbis; p. 36 Sipa Press/Rex Features; p. 42 89 Studio/Shutterstock; p. 43 Meawpong 34 05/Shutterstock. Every attempt has been made to clear copyright for this edition. Should there be any inadvertent omission please apply to the publisher for rectification.

Contents

CHAPTER 1
Birth of a New Brand

Facebook is one of the biggest and most recognizable brands in the world. More than 500 million people in 180 countries are members of the site, and the numbers are growing every day. There was even a movie released in 2010, *The Social Network*, starring Justin Timberlake and Jesse Eisenberg, about the founders of Facebook.

Mark Zuckerberg launched Facebook from his dorm room in Kirkland House at Harvard in 2004.

Brains Behind the Brand

Mark Zuckerberg – Founder and chief executive officer (CEO)
As CEO of Facebook, Mark is the man at the top. He is responsible for setting the company's overall direction and product strategy, and he is the driving force behind everything Facebook does now and hopes to do in the future. A CEO's role includes everything from marketing, strategy, financing, the creation of company culture, human resources, hiring, firing, sales, public relations (PR) and so on. In 2010, Mark won *TIME* magazine's Person of the Year award.

> " [My Harvard roommates] and I would sit around and talk... about how we thought that the added transparency in the world, all the added access to information and sharing would inevitably change big world things. But we had no idea we would play a part in it... We were just a group of college kids. "
>
> *Mark Zuckerberg*

The company is the brainchild of Mark Zuckerberg, who launched the site as a 19-year-old computer science student at prestigious Harvard University in Cambridge, MA.

Mark and a few of his fellow students had grown frustrated at Harvard's refusal to put a list of the university's students (the "facebooks" kept by each of Harvard's 12 undergraduate houses) online. So Mark hacked into the university's records, gaining access to students' personal details and photographs, and created Facemash — a program that allowed people to vote on who were the best-looking students at Harvard!

Mark wrote the program from scratch in one eight-hour programming session — eventually finishing it at 4:00 AM on Sunday November 2, 2003. Mark launched the site mid-afternoon that day and e-mailed links to a few friends. By 10:30 PM the site had been visited by 450 students, who had voted on 22,000 pairs of photos!

Harvard professors discovered the project, and forced Mark to close it down. He was called before the university's disciplinary committee and put on probation. But most important, Mark had discovered he had the ability to create software that people couldn't stop using. The idea behind Facebook was born.

The ad for the film The Social Network *about Facebook, released in 2010 and featuring actor Jesse Eisenberg as Mark Zuckerberg.*

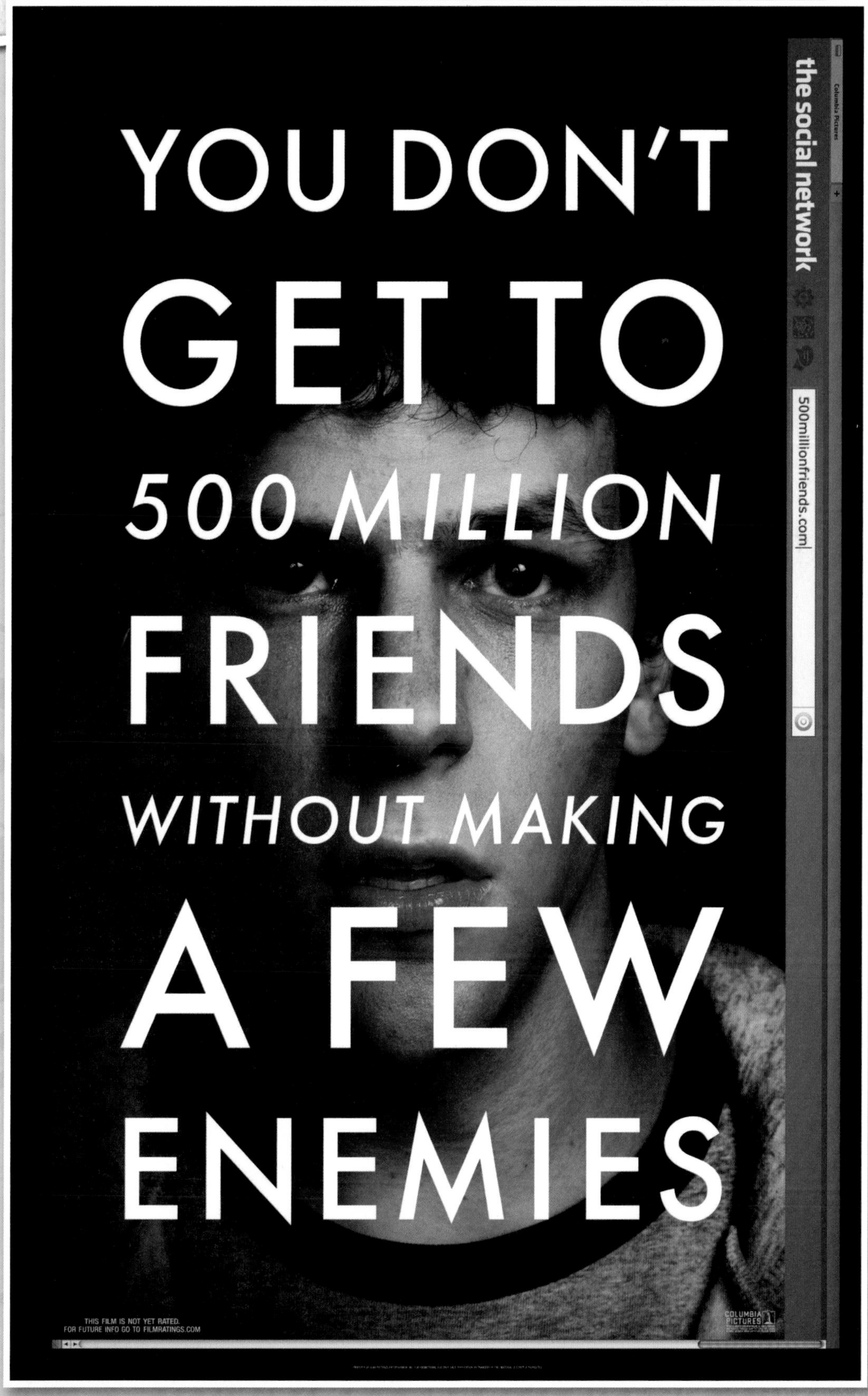
YOU DON'T
GET TO
500 MILLION
FRIENDS
WITHOUT MAKING
A FEW
ENEMIES
the social network
500millionfriends.com
Columbia Pictures
THIS FILM IS NOT YET RATED.
FOR FUTURE INFO GO TO FILMRATINGS.COM
COLUMBIA PICTURES

CHAPTER 2

Facebook, Inc.

After the success of Facemash, Mark decided to keep working on Web sites that explored social connections. On January 11, 2004, he registered the domain name www.Thefacebook.com. It cost $35 for one year.

The site Mark wanted to build borrowed ideas from Facemash, as well as a service called Friendster, a dating Web site that was extremely popular at Harvard at the time. Friendster allowed users to build a profile of themselves online and include information about hobbies, musical tastes and other personal information.

Mark had launched Facemash from his laptop, but he knew he would need a more powerful computer to host Thefacebook. He signed up with an online company called Manage.com to host the site on its computers (known as servers).

▼ *An early Thefacebook.com page from 2004 belonging to a Harvard student, Melissa Doman.*

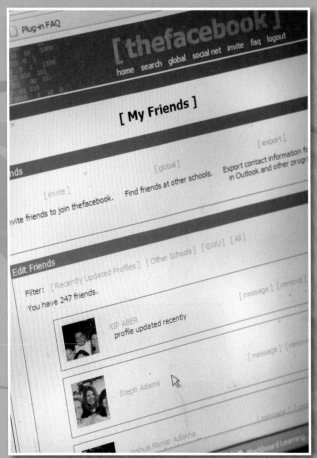

Business Matters

Forming a company — A limited or incorporated company is a business owned by shareholders (people who own shares in the company), and run by directors.

The company's shares have a basic value, for example $1 each, which stays the same, and a market value, which goes up and down depending on how good an investment the shares are judged to be by people outside the company who want to buy those shares.

As well as investing money in Thefacebook, Eduardo helped Mark figure out how to make money from the site.

Mark also made a deal with a Harvard classmate named Eduardo Saverin, giving him one-third of the company in exchange for Eduardo investing $1,000 in Thefacebook. At this time, Thefacebook was not legally incorporated (see Business Matters, p. 8); it was simply a company name, registered by Mark, with big ideas for the future.

On February 4, 2004, Thefacebook.com went live. The home screen read: "Thefacebook is an online directory that connects people through social networks at colleges. We have opened up Thefacebook for popular consumption at Harvard University. You can use Thefacebook to: Search for people at your school; Find out who is in your classes; Look up your friends' friends; See a visualization of your social network."

> Facebook's software makes information viral. Ideas and trends have the ability to rush through groups and make people aware of something almost simultaneously — like a virus. The Facebook Effect can create a sudden interest in a news story, a song or a YouTube video.
>
> **David Kirkpatrick, author of The Facebook Effect**

Personal Information

The way Facebook works is simple and has changed very little since its launch as Thefacebook.com in 2004. To sign up, you create a profile with your personal information and a photo of yourself. You can indicate your

▼ *Christopher Cox, vice president of product, speaks at the TechCrunch Disrupt conference in New York in 2010. Cox is responsible for organizing Facebook's new product launches.*

relationship status — single, married, etc. — and can include your birthday and the city or town where you live. In the "Info" section, you can tell people many things such as which school you go to and your favorite books.

Privacy Controls

Privacy controls allow you to decide who sees your information, from your date of birth to your religious views, to photos and videos you are tagged in. You also have the option to customize access to different parts of your page.

The Wall

This feature was added in September 2004, and it allows anyone to write whatever they want straight onto your profile. It can be a message to you or a comment about you. Any visitor to your profile can see it, and comment.

Create Group

This feature was also added in September 2004. It allows users to create a group to represent an interest of theirs — a fan page for a film or band, for example. Each group has its own page, like a regular user profile.

Photos

Toward the end of 2005, photo-hosting Web sites like Flickr were exploding on the Internet. Facebook decided to allow users to upload unlimited numbers of photos and also had the idea of allowing users to "tag" them — in other words, to list the names of their Facebook friends in the pictures and link to their pages.

Within a month of the launch, 85 percent of Facebook users had been tagged in at least one photo. Facebook is now by far the Web's largest photo-sharing site, with 48 billion images stored, and 1 million more added every week!

News Feed

Launched in autumn 2006, this allows you to see all your friends' updates in real time, by clicking on the Facebook logo in the top left-hand corner of your profile page. Even the smallest pieces of information keep users hooked.

Inbox

Facebook's internal e-mail service between site users was one of the original features of the site when it was launched.

Chat

Facebook's instant messaging service was launched in April 2008, allowing users to communicate with friends in the same way as services like Microsoft's MSN and AOL's AIM.

▼ *This is an example of a Facebook page today.*

Business Matters

Market research - All successful companies must understand the market in which they are operating and the actions of their competitors. For Facebook, this means understanding what the site's users want and what other social networking sites are offering. They watch the market closely and take note of any changes. For example, when people started spending more time online through their mobile phones, Facebook launched a mobile service.

Marketing — Marketing is a process that attempts to understand the market and its requirements (in Facebook's case, the users and what they want from the site), so that the company only provides products or services that the market wants. Marketing creates demand within the market, thereby minimizing the selling activity required. Much of Facebook's success comes from word of mouth — satisfied user talking to satisfied user.

CHAPTER 4
The Idea Keeps on Growing

By the end of Thefacebook's first week of launch, about half of all Harvard undergraduates had signed up, and by the end of February 2004 about 6,000 people were active users.

Mark realized that he had to quickly expand outside Harvard to take advantage of the interest in the site and to stay ahead of the competition. He employed his roommate Dustin Moskowitz as an extra programmer. It was Dustin's job to make the Web site available to other universities.

With Dustin's help, the site launched very quickly at other prestigious US universities, including those in the "Ivy League." Thefacebook launched at Columbia and Stanford on February 25, 2004, and at Yale on February 29. Dartmouth and Cornell followed on March 7 and then Massachusetts Institute of Technology (MIT), University of Pennsylvania, Princeton, Brown and Boston University were added soon afterward.

By the end of May 2004, Thefacebook was not only operating at Harvard (shown here). It had spread to 34 colleges and had almost 100,000 users.

Brains Behind the Brand

Dustin Moskowitz – Cofounder of Facebook

Dustin (born May 22, 1984) was one of Mark Zuckerberg's three roommates at Harvard and one of the cofounders of Facebook. As the Web site grew in popularity at Harvard, Dustin — who was studying economics — taught himself computer programming so that he could help Mark quickly expand to other universities. As the company grew, Dustin led the technical and engineering divisions. He left the company in 2008 to start his own company, but he still owns around 6 percent of Facebook's stock.

Within a month of the launch, Thefacebook had 10,000 active users. By the end of March, the total number of users had reached 30,000! By then, Mark was spending $450 per month on servers with Manage.com to cope with all the Web traffic, and he and Eduardo agreed to put another $10,000 each into the company. Thefacebook was growing rapidly, yet there were no signs of income for the Web site. Mark was offered $10 million for the company in June, but he turned the offer down.

A Yale Facebook page.

Business Matters

The Unique Selling Proposition or Point (USP) — A USP is some unique quality about a company's product or service that will attract customers to use or buy it rather than an alternative product from a competitor. Facebook stood out from competitors like Friendster and even MySpace because of its functionality (what it could do), its appearance (how it looked) and its quality (how it worked).

Eduardo arranged a meeting with Y2M, a company that sold ads for college newspaper Web sites. It was amazed at the site's traffic and agreed to use it to place ads for its clients. One of the first ads was for a special MasterCard credit card for students. MasterCard didn't believe Thefacebook could deliver results, so it agreed to pay only when a student filled out an application. Within a day it had received twice the applications it had expected to get in four months! Mark didn't like advertising on the site, but he knew they needed it to make money. Sometimes he put a caption above the ads saying, "We don't like these either but they pay the bills."

CHAPTER 5

An Expert on Board

For the summer break in 2004, Mark rented a house in Palo Alto, California, to be close to Silicon Valley. He convinced Dustin to join him, along with two Harvard students who came along for work experience.

Every day, Mark and the other programmers would sleep late, getting up after lunch, and then meet in the dining room and work on programming additions to the site until past midnight.

In Palo Alto, Mark met Sean Parker. Sean had helped launch a famous music-sharing Web site called Napster in 1999, and he was convinced that social networking was "the hot new thing." The pair got along very well, and Mark valued Sean's business experience. Sean was a great talker, a confident deal maker and experienced in the ways of Silicon Valley. Mark was soon calling Sean "the company president."

With Sean Parker's help, Thefacebook started to become a properly structured and organized company. Rather than use Manage.com's servers, they bought their own, and employed an operations manager to make sure everything ran smoothly. Mark's biggest worry was that the numbers of users might slow down the site and make visitors annoyed and impatient with the service. These problems had caused big companies like Friendster to lose users and eventually fail.

Sean Parker's growing influence caused problems with Eduardo Saverin, who fell out with Mark and eventually left the company. But Mark remained committed to seeing Thefacebook grow. That summer he and his parents invested $85,000 of their own money into the company for new servers to keep the site running quickly. The money was originally intended to pay for Mark's continuing Harvard education.

◄ *Sean Parker left Facebook a year after becoming the president after differences of opinion with other board members.*

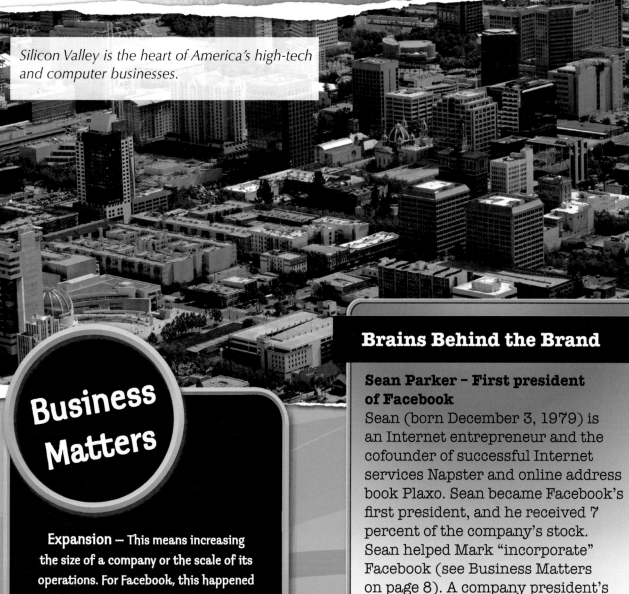

Silicon Valley is the heart of America's high-tech and computer businesses.

Business Matters

Expansion — This means increasing the size of a company or the scale of its operations. For Facebook, this happened when it expanded beyond Harvard so that other universities and eventually everyone in the world could use it. Expansion can make a business more profitable as well as more cost-efficient, by increasing profits but keeping certain costs — like wages and office rent — the same.

Brains Behind the Brand

Sean Parker – First president of Facebook

Sean (born December 3, 1979) is an Internet entrepreneur and the cofounder of successful Internet services Napster and online address book Plaxo. Sean became Facebook's first president, and he received 7 percent of the company's stock. Sean helped Mark "incorporate" Facebook (see Business Matters on page 8). A company president's main responsibilities are to ensure that all lines of business are running efficiently and within a budget set by the board of directors. The president also usually works with senior-level managers to devise plans that will generate revenues, create new business opportunities, and help the company remain competitive in the marketplace.

CHAPTER 6
Making Popularity Pay

By the end of the summer, the Web site had grown to over 200,000 users.
It was becoming so big and time-consuming that Mark and Dustin decided to leave
college to concentrate on it full time. The cost of running the new company was arou
$50,000 per month, and income just wasn't keeping up.

PayPal's advertising partner Y2M brought Paramount Pictures on board to promote the new SpongeBob SquarePants film on Thefacebook.

Thefacebook needed funding fast, so Sean Parker arranged a meeting with Peter Thiel, a well-known Silicon Valley investor, and the man who cofounded a successful Web payments site called PayPal. Peter agreed to give $500,000 for 10.2 percent of the company (this valued all of Thefacebook at $4.9 million).

Business Matters

Company shareholders — Shareholders at companies like Facebook hope to make money in two ways. First, as the company makes money, the value of its shares will rise, so an investor can make a profit if he or she sells his or her shares (known as a capital gain). Second, part of the profit that a company makes every year can be given to shareholders based on how many shares they own. This is called a dividend.

facebook | Search

Fans of Apple 👍 Like

| **Wall** | Info | Photos | Discussions | Not |

Fans of Apple + others | Just Fans of Apple | Just ot

Fans of Apple How true do you think this i

📷 about an hour ago · Share

👍 118 people like this.

💬 View all 35 comments

Fans of Apple

Facebook's most popular Apple fan page with *over* 200K fans!

⌄ **suggest us!**

Suggest to friends

Are YOU an Apple fanatic and obsessed with Steve Jobs and his NEXT great innovation? If so, you're in the right place ... so JOIN today!!!

Information

Founded:
April 1, 1976

238,765 people like this

Fans of Apple Mark Zuckerberg said at th
that the iPad (with 95% of the tablet marke
doesn't need a dedicated app because ther
and let Mark know what you think.

Yesterday at 02:18

👍 58 people like this.

💬 View all 85 comments

Fans of Apple Australian iPad/iPhone use
business (Source: http://delimiter.com.au/
ibookstore-floodgates/)

Wednesday at 02:27

Apple followed Paramount and created a special fan page for fans of Apple.

ok Mobile event
e as an iPhone and
ets. Speak up below

re is now open for
le-australia-opens-

In the first week of the new college term, Mark and his team of programmers added 15 new colleges. In September 2004, membership doubled to around 400,000, and it reached half a million on October 21. Even with Peter Thiel's investment, Mark knew he would have to put more time and effort into finding advertisers to help bring in cash.

Paramount Pictures pioneered a new concept that would become critical to Facebook's growth — creating a special "group" for fans of a film. Apple was the next big company to sign up, paying Facebook $1 for every new user who joined their group, with a monthly guarantee of $50,000. Facebook had started to solve the problem of how to make its popularity pay!

By April 2005, Sean Parker had negotiated another round of funding for the fast-growing company. Accel Partners agreed to invest $12.7 million, valuing Thefacebook at $98 million. This valuation amazed the business world, as even Google's first big investment valued Google at $75 million!

With the money from Accel Partners, Mark could build a real team and turn Thefacebook into a global brand.

To High School and Beyond

In the summer of 2005, Mark bought the domain name Facebook.com, and the company finally became Facebook as it is known today on September 20, 2005.

The Facebook company employs over 1,000 people.

With an amazing 85 percent of US college students already Facebook users, the company decided to open up its service to the country's 37,000 high schools.

The move was a huge success. By April 2006 there were 1 million high school users. A lot of Facebook employees were worried that college students would be put off by having high school kids on "their" Web site, but actually the feedback was that university students enjoyed being able to communicate with a larger network of potential friends.

Mark had gambled and won. Now he was ready to take on the world, and Facebook expanded its service again in September 2006. Called "open registration," it opened

Charting the growth of Facebook from its launch at Harvard to its first 1 million users and beyond.

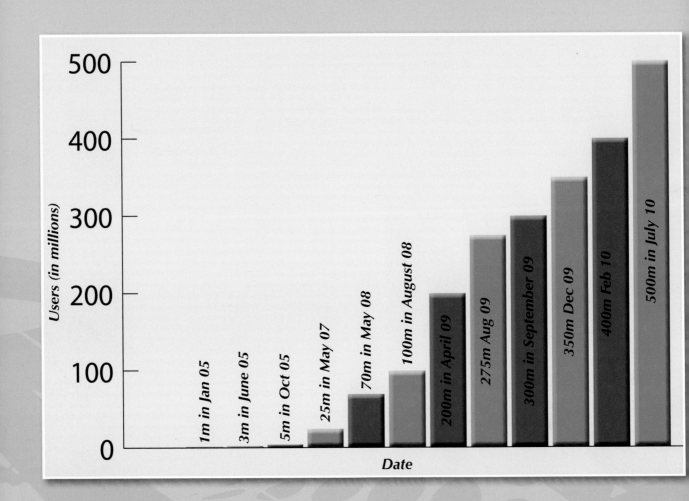

Users (in millions)

- 1m in Jan 05
- 3m in June 05
- 5m in Oct 05
- 25m in May 07
- 70m in May 08
- 100m in August 08
- 200m in April 09
- 275m Aug 09
- 300m in September 09
- 350m Dec 09
- 400m Feb 10
- 500m in July 10

Date

the site up to everyone around the world over the age of 13 with an e-mail address. New users started joining at a rate of 50,000 per day. The Facebook brand had become hugely popular and recognizable to millions. Revenue (or money coming in to the company) had risen to $1 million per month. Unfortunately, costs were $1.5 million per month! Luckily, Facebook came to an agreement with software company Microsoft, which agreed to use its own sales team to sell ads on Facebook pages.

Business Matters

Branding — All the qualities and features of a product, including its name and its appearance, are presented to the customer as a brand. To be successful, all brands — from Facebook to McDonald's to Nike — need to be distinctive (stand out in some way from competitors), consistent (always provide the same level of quality, and therefore be seen as reliable), recognizable (through a logo or "look" of a product) and attractive. The blue Facebook logo has become as recognizable as a Nike swoosh.

The deal, which guaranteed Facebook $100 million in revenue for 2007, accounted for over half of the site's revenue, and turned it into a profitable company for the first time.

In October 2007, Microsoft bought 1.6 percent of Facebook for $240 million, valuing the company at $15 billion.

CHAPTER 8

Going Global

Facebook is a global and recognizable brand.

By the start of 2008, 70 percent of Facebook's 145 million active users were outside the US. However, the site was in English. This meant that most of the ads on the site were irrelevant. Worse still, it couldn't make money. To deal with this problem, Facebook decided to launch international-language versions of the site.

The Facebook login page in Chinese.

It also had the innovative idea of asking site users to get involved with translating it into other languages. Fifteen hundred Spanish speakers helped create a Spanish version in just four weeks. The German site took 2,000 people just two weeks. The French site was launched in just two days with the help of 4,000 people!

At the end of 2008, Facebook had grown to 350 million users around the world, and it could be used in 35 languages. It was growing at a rate of 1 million new users per day in 180 countries.

Facebook now operates in over 70 languages — from Afrikaans to Zulu — and covers 98 percent of the world's population. In some key countries like Japan, China, Russia, Korea and Brazil, it still lags behind local networking sites. However, the site has become a huge global success and is always trying to increase its market share. In India, for example, Facebook won thousands of new users by working with the Indian Premier League (IPL) to build a fan page for its annual cricket tournament on the site.

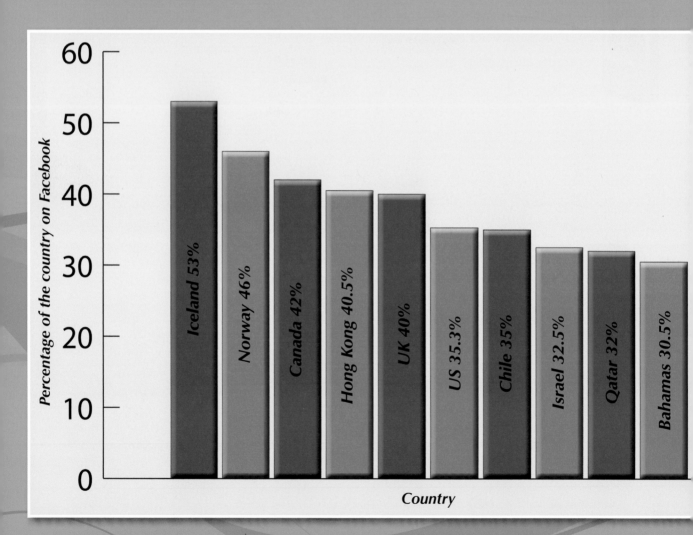

In 17 countries, more than 30 percent of the whole country is on Facebook!

Business Matters

Critical mass – This is when a company expands until it achieves a strength or dominance in any particular market (or in Facebook's case, country) that means it achieves automatic brand recognition and can effectively control the market. For example, one in every two people wanting to join a social network in Iceland choose Facebook.

International expansion has also caused problems. All of Facebook's servers — the computers that host all 500 million users' Facebook profiles — are housed in two data centers in the United States. This means that pages can take a long time to load and refresh, the farther a country is from the United States. Facebook is investing in several expensive new "data farms" around the world, as well as opening international offices, to cope with increased demand.

CHAPTER 9
The Secret to Making Money

Sheryl Sandberg brought brand advertising to Facebook.

In March 2008, Mark hired executive Sheryl Sandberg from rival Google. He gave her one specific task — turn Facebook into a long-lasting, money-making business.

Sheryl had helped Google build its advertising into a multimillion-dollar business, and she was convinced that Facebook was an even better environment for advertisers. Whereas Google's search engine helped people find the things they had already decided they wanted to buy, Facebook could help people decide what they wanted.

Brand advertising, like in the ads on television and on Facebook, puts a new idea in your head — a film to see at the movies, a breakfast cereal to buy. The advertising industry spends 80 percent of its money — or $480 billion annually — on these types of ads. Online ads are becoming more popular as the Internet draws people away from the traditional media of newspapers, magazines and TV. Increasingly important

Brains Behind the Brand

Sheryl Sandberg – Chief operating officer (COO)

Sheryl was a prize-winning student of economics at Harvard. She graduated with an MBA from Harvard Business School and then worked as chief of staff for the US Treasury Department under President Bill Clinton. From there she joined Google, where she managed online sales channels and consumer products worldwide. Sheryl joined Facebook in 2008 to oversee all the company's sales, marketing, business development and human resources. She has been named as one of the "50 Most Powerful Women in Business" by *Fortune* magazine.

This is an ad board on Facebook, geared toward users in the UK.

facebook | Search 🔍

Advert board

FREE Samples - Nov. 5th ✕
epicdirectnetwork.com

Major brands are giving away free samples. Fill in your email address and get yours today. Hurry - today's free samples will go fast!

Dresses Under £20 ✕
bonprixsecure.com

Huge range of dresses. Shop now at Bonprix UK!

Burberry ✕

Click 'Like' to join the official Burberry Fan Page and view our new Winter Storms collection.

👍 Like

Toftcombs House-
toftcombsmans

Toftcombs Man due to cancella year . Sleeps 1 acres of beauti Borders.

£29 Warwickshire Hotel ✕
travelzoo.com

Deal at Grade II-listed hotel includes breakfast, 3-course dinner, upgrade & free drinks. Get this deal by email before it sells out

adidas® - 30% off Sale ✕
shop.adidas.co.uk

Save a massive 30% on a huge selection of trainers & clothes! offer ends soon. Shop at the Official adidas

Fantastic Tampons! ✕

Introducing Trinkets. Gorgeous tampons delivered monthly so you'll never run out again. Sign up now and get your 1st box free!

Andrex Pup

Hi! I'm the Andr and I'm making friends on Face and join us – pr now!

👍 Like

Increasingly important to Facebook are what are called self-service ads — ads that small businesses can buy with a credit card through the site (www.facebook.com/ advertising). Because Facebook holds so much information about each of its users, advertisers — particularly local advertisers — are able to target their customers very accurately. If you have a restaurant in Philadelphia, for example, you don't have to waste money advertising to people in Chicago or Los Angeles. You can target potential customers based on location, age and even their tastes in food!

Home   Profile   Account ▾

Create an advert

ow to Lose
tomach Fat   ×
ealthcastle.com

is popular site shows
rprising (healthy) foods
at help to burn stomach fat
nd erase unwanted pounds
ily by using this diet tip

niversity of
iverpool   ×
line-studies.net

ve over 3 years of
perience in your
ofession? This is your
ance to take your masters

Business Matters

Advertising sales – The two main ways that Facebook makes money from ads are cost per thousand views (CPM) and cost per acquisition (CPA). Companies like Apple and Victoria's Secret use CPA, paying Facebook $1 per month for every member who joins their fan pages. Other companies who target specific groups — for example, university students or single people ages 25-30 — use CPM, paying an agreed price in order to be seen on these people's pages. Rates start at $5 per thousand views for these ads. With 500 million users viewing the home page many times a month, this quickly adds up!

The number of advertisers using this service tripled from 2008 to 2009. In 2009, Facebook made $300-400 million from its self-service ad program — by far the highest share of the company's ad revenue.

CHAPTER 10

There's More to Facebook Than Friends

From its earliest days, Mark Zuckerberg wanted Facebook to be more than just a place where people went to communicate. He wanted it to be a "platform" encouraging outside software developers to design applications for the site.

Becoming a platform is what every technology company dreams of. Microsoft dominated the technology business for 20 years by positioning its Windows software as the number-one operating system platform for the PC industry.

If a new generation of computer programmers used Facebook as the basis for their programs, it would ensure that the Web site stayed relevant and useful for years to come. What's more, the better the features that exist on Facebook, the more irreplaceable the site becomes in people's lives.

In business, there is something called a "Eureka moment," when a company sees very clearly what is — and what isn't — its core business, and therefore where it should direct its resources and energies. Facebook's "social network," its fast and simple connections to all your friends, had created what Mark described as "the most powerful distribution mechanism that has been created in a generation." He decided that what Facebook did best was maintain your personal profile and your network of friend connections. The rest he would leave to outside software companies to invent.

Mark Zuckerberg introduces new features for Facebook during a keynote speech at f8, a one-day developer conference, sponsored by Facebook in 2010.

Again, his plan was a great success. Facebook Platform allows developers to create applications that interact with Facebook. It was launched in May 2007, and more than one million developers from 180 countries have programmed applications for Facebook — from electronic pet favorite Fluff Friends to games like Farmville and Mafia Wars.

News Feed announcements were the perfect way of learning what applications your friends had downloaded, and within six months of the launch, half of Facebook users had at least one application on their profile. The result? More time spent on the site, and more connections being made.

Business Matters

Diversification — Companies often decide to offer new products or services — like the games on Facebook — because this reduces the risk of its other products becoming too limited or uninteresting. By allowing developers to add games and applications, Facebook was providing an extra reason for users to visit the site. When companies offer a completely different product or service, like Facebook's alternative to PayPal for buying products online, or supermarkets offering car or house insurance, it is called brand stretching.

Brains Behind the Brand

Chamath Palihapitiya - Vice president of growth, mobile and international
Chamath graduated as an electrical engineer, before spending five years working for Web site AOL (America Online), where he became vice president and general manager of its instant messaging service, AIM. At Facebook, Chamath is responsible for increasing the number of site users, both on the Web and on mobile devices. Previously, he helped launch Facebook Platform and led the team that built the self-service ads program.

Kingdoms of Camelot is a popular Facebook game.

CHAPTER 11
To Share or Not to Share?

Five hundred million users post their relationship status, their photos, even their dates of birth and mobile phone numbers on their pages. Like any company that holds this kind of data on its users, Facebook has a duty to keep it from falling into the wrong hands.

However, the site was established as a way of sharing information. It's this contradiction that has sometimes caused problems.

From time to time, changes to Facebook's default (standard) settings have resulted in users' profiles becoming completely open to all the site's users and not just to their chosen friends. In other words, information is marked "public" unless a user manually changes it to "private." On these occasions, angry user groups spring up to protest the changes, and Facebook points out what needs to be done to regain your privacy.

The question is, should Facebook settings actually be set to "private," but give users the ability to make them "public," rather than vice versa? With Mark Zuckerberg's passion for openness, this seems unlikely, but this is a problem that the Web site will need to tackle.

◄ *Dan Rose directs product marketing for Facebook.*

In May 2010, the site received an official complaint in the United States from the Electronic Privacy Information Center, which highlighted the complicated and often confusing privacy controls.

One reason for Facebook's desire to keep users' information public comes down to money. The site makes your information available — for a fee — to advertisers, who then use it to aim specific, targeted products at you through your profile page.

In addition, Facebook has recently signed valuable contracts with search engines Google and Microsoft's Bing to allow status updates that are not set to private to be accessed for more accurate searches.

Thanks to Facebook, social networking has become very big business. Mark Zuckerberg and his management team have to work out how to keep everyone happy — advertisers and users — if they are going to enjoy the same huge growth that they have experienced over the last five years.

> " The concept that the world will be better if we share more is something that's pretty foreign to a lot of people... To get people to this point where there's more openness — that's a big challenge, but I think we'll do it. "
>
> *Mark Zuckerberg*

▼ *Facebook's privacy settings allow users to decide what information they make public and what they keep private.*

Brains Behind the Brand

Dan Rose – Vice president of partnerships and platform marketing

Dan joined Facebook in 2006 from Amazon.com, where he helped develop the Kindle electronic book reader. At Facebook, Dan is in charge of product marketing for Facebook Platform (see p.p. 34-35). Platform allows software developers from outside Facebook to create for the site, increasing its usefulness to users. Dan is also responsible for the company's mergers and acquisitions — in other words, researching other companies for Facebook to buy to strengthen and grow its own business.

Today, Facebook employs 1,400 people — from its headquarters in Palo Alto, California, to centers in Dublin, Sydney and Tokyo, among others.

From humble beginnings, company revenues are estimated to reach $1 billion in 2010. Each month 25 billion pieces of content are posted on the site — from Web links to news stories and photos. As of February 2010, the site had more than 400 million active users — over 25 percent of the people on the Internet worldwide — with numbers growing at 25 million per month.

The signs look good for Facebook's continued success. In March 2009 it was reported that time spent on social networks by Internet users worldwide had for the first time exceeded the

> " [Facebook] is a platform for people to get more out of their lives. It is a new form of communication, just as was instant messaging, e-mail, the telephone, and the telegraph. "
>
> **David Kirkpatrick, author of The Facebook Effect**

Business Matters

Long-term success — Successful companies are market-driven. In other words, they focus on satisfying the exact section of the market in which they are operating. All of Facebook's divisions — from programming to new product development — have to make sure that they create something that the site's visitors ("the market") want. Successful companies also need to be "sustainable," meaning that people not only want to buy or use their products now, but that they will continue to want to use them in the future.

You can take your phone anywhere, so Facebook users on their mobile phones are twice as active as non-mobile users.

amount of time spent on e-mail. Time spent on Facebook increased 566 percent to 20.5 billion minutes per year, and 50 percent of active users log on every day.

Where will Facebook go from here? One way it is continuing to expand is on mobile devices. Facebook Mobile is now supported by 200 mobile operators in 60 different countries, and more than 150 million people currently access the site through their phones. Just as encouraging for Facebook is the fact that it is now attracting older users. The site's fastest-growing demographic, or age group, is now "over-34-year-olds," who make up 28 percent of the site's users.

And finally, Facebook is making itself an integral part of your life even when you're not on the site!

A new initiative called Open Graph, launched in April 2010, integrates the Facebook "Likes" thumbs-up onto 100,000 outside Web sites, allowing Facebook users to express their opinions on everything from a newspaper story to a pair of jeans. What better way to get recommendations on what film to see, or what sneakers to buy than from 500 million people?

Mark Zuckerberg presents Facebook's plans for long-term success.

To create a new product, it is helpful to put together a product development brief like the one below. This is a sample brief for the Facebook Life Saver app. SWOT analysis on the page opposite helps you to think about the strengths, weaknesses, opportunities and threats of your product. This can help you to see how feasible and practical your idea is before you think of investing in it.

Product Development Brief

Name of application: Facebook Life Saver

Design of logo:

The product explained (use 25 words or less): Ever spent too long on Facebook? Our application can be set to sound an alarm after a preset time. Get your life back!

Target age of users: 10-100

What does the product do? The product is a simple alarm that users can set when they log on to their Facebook page. They can then forget about it - until it sounds! It's for all those people who plan to go on Facebook for ten minutes and are still there three hours later!

Are there any similar products already available? Not that I know of.

What makes your product different? I have looked at a lot of different Facebook applications, from games to friends and family to lifestyle, and I haven't found anything like this. It's easy to use, and it's fun, so lots of people will be talking about it!

Name of Facebook application you are assessing: Facebook Life Saver
The table below will help you assess your Facebook application. By addressing all four areas, you can make your application stronger and more likely to be a success.

Questions to consider

Does your application do something unique?

What are its USPs (unique selling points)?

Why will people use this application instead of a different application?

Strengths

No similar applications are currently available.

It has novelty value and does the opposite of what you would expect, that is, it tells you to get OFF Facebook rather than stay on. People will talk about it.

Why wouldn't people use this application?

Does it work on all kinds of computers — PCs and Macs?

Is it as good or better than other similar applications already available?

Weaknesses

People enjoy spending time on Facebook and maybe don't want to be reminded that they should stop!

There's only me to answer queries or problems, so people might have to wait a few hours for a response.

Will the issue that the application tackles become more important over time?

Will new markets emerge for this application?

Can the application target new niche (small, specific) markets?

Can it be used globally?

Can it develop new USPs?

Opportunities

I think the issue of spending too much time on Facebook and other social networks will become more important in the future.

Other social networks are likely to pop up, and hopefully they can offer the same application.

It can be used around the world, as everyone knows what a clock face is.

Is the market (i.e. Facebook) shrinking? Are people moving to other social networks?

Will new technology make your application unnecessary?

Are any of your weaknesses so bad that they might affect the application in the long run?

Is Facebook likely to decide to remove applications from the site?

Threats

Facebook might decide to do something like this themselves and build it into Facebook.

Facebook might decide they want people to spend more time on the site and remove the application.

Do You Have What It Takes to Work at Facebook? Try This!

1) Do you like school?
a) Not really, I prefer weekends and vacations.
b) It's OK. I like a few subjects like English and history, but I don't like science and math.
c) Yes, I like to get good grades, and I don't mind putting in a little extra work to achieve them.

2) How often do you use the Internet?
a) Never. I only use the computer to watch DVDs.
b) Not very often. Just to e-mail my homework into school.
c) All the time! I use it to do research for homework and to have fun.

3) What kind of Web sites do you look at?
a) I've seen a few YouTube videos that friends have recommended.
b) A few. Amazon and eBay for some shopping, and Hulu to catch up on favorite TV programs.
c) Loads! I like gaming sites, as well as Flickr and Facebook, and I'm always searching for new, fun sites.

4) Do you use the Internet to talk and connect to friends?
a) No, that's what the phone is for.
b) Yes, I sometimes use AIM.
c) All the time! I even have the laptop on while I'm watching TV so that I can keep talking to my friends.

5) How often do you use Facebook?
a) Never. I keep meaning to set up a profile, but I haven't gotten around to it.
b) Occasionally. I have a profile, but I haven't updated it for ages!
c) Regularly. I talk to my friends on Facebook Chat, and I'm always uploading new pictures and joining new groups.

6) If you could suggest one improvement to the site, what would it be?
a) I'd like to see a different logo. I don't like the color blue.
b) I'd like to see some games on there. Oh, have they done that already?
c) Where do I start? I'd like a program that tells me to log on because my friends have just gone online — like a "News Flash."

Results

Mostly As: Sorry, but your chances of working at Facebook are looking shaky! It doesn't sound like you have the interest in the Internet or social networking to succeed at this world-famous company.

Mostly Bs: You are interested in computers and the Internet, but you need to work on your motivation and drive to succeed in a very competitive business.

Mostly Cs: It sounds like you have what it takes to get a job at Facebook! Keep working hard at school, and keep using and enjoying social networking sites, and who knows?

Glossary

acquisition The act of buying or taking ownership of something, usually a company.

customize To modify or build according to personal specifications or preference.

diversify To vary products and services in order to expand or to spread risk.

dominate To control, rule over or govern.

entrepreneur A person who organizes and manages a business, usually with considerable initiative and risk.

exceed To excel; be superior to; surpass.

from scratch From the very beginning or start.

graduate To receive a university degree.

hack into To gain entry into a computer program, usually in order to change it.

humble Low in importance or status.

innovative Using or showing new methods or ideas.

irreplaceable Unique; impossible to replace.

lag behind To move or develop more slowly than competitors toward a goal or objective.

Mac Apple Macintosh. There are several lines of Apple Macintosh computers that have been designed and produced by the Apple company.

market share The percentage of a market that a company controls.

minimize To reduce to the smallest possible amount.

on probation Under supervision following a past offense to avoid future wrongdoing.

PC Personal computer. PCs are general all-purpose computers.

post To put information online.

prestigious Respected; with a good reputation.

revenue A company's income before costs are taken into account; gross income.

Silicon Valley Region in the San Francisco Bay Area of Northern California. It is home to many of the world's largest technology corporations.

strategy A plan or method for achieving a particular result or goal.

tag To link photographs on Facebook with a name. This personal identification means that the tagged subject of the photo is alerted through Facebook about the presence of the image.

transparency Openness; clarity.

unique One of a kind; unequalled.

For More Information

Berkman Center for Internet & Society at Harvard University

23 Everett Street, 2nd Floor
Cambridge, MA 02138
(617) 495-7547
Web site: http://cyber.law.harvard.edu

The Berkman Center was founded to explore cyberspace, share in its study, and help pioneer its development. The center represents a network of academics, students, and professionals working to identify and engage with the challenges and opportunities of cyberspace.

Facebook, Inc.

1601 S. California Avenue
Palo Alto, CA 94304
(650) 543-4800
Web site: http://www.facebook.com

Facebook's mission is to give people the power to share and make the world more open and connected. Millions of people use Facebook every day to keep up with friends, upload photos, share links and videos, and learn more about the people they meet.

Information and Privacy Commissioner (IPC) of Ontario, Canada

2 Bloor Street East, Suite 1400
Toronto, ON M4W 1A8
Canada
(800) 387-0073
Web site: http://www.ipc.on.ca

The IPC works independently from the Canadian government to protect personal privacy and call awareness to the issue.

Mashable

121 East 24th Street
New York, NY 10003
(646) 397-0874
Web site: http://www.mashable.com

Mashable is an independent news source dedicated to covering digital culture, social media and technology. Mashable reports on the importance of digital innovation and how it empowers and inspires people around the world.

Media Awareness Network (MNet)

950 Gladstone Avenue, Suite 120
Ottawa, ON K1Y 3E6
Canada
(613) 224-7721
Web site: http://www.media-awareness.ca

MNet is a Canadian nonprofit organization that promotes media literacy and digital literacy by producing education and awareness programs and resources.

Pew Internet & American Life Project

Pew Research Center
1615 L Street NW, Suite 700
Washington, DC 20036

The Pew Internet & American Life Project conducts original research that explores the impact of the Internet on children, families, communities, the workplace, schools, health care and civic and political life. It seeks to be an authoritative source for timely information on the Internet's growth and societal impact.

Web Sites

Due to the changing nature of Internet links, Rosen Publishing has developed an online list of Web sites related to the subject of this book. This site is updated regularly. Please use this link to access the list:

http://www.rosenlinks.com/bht/face

Hasday, Judy L. *Facebook and Mark Zuckerberg* (Business Leaders). Greensboro, NC: Morgan Reynolds Publishing, 2012.

Hill, Z. B. *Mark Zuckerberg: From Facebook to Famous* (Extraordinary Success with a High School Diploma or Less). Broomall, PA: Mason Crest Publishers, 2012.

Hillstrom, Laurie Collier. *Online Social Networks* (Technology 360). Detroit, MI: Lucent Books, 2010.

Kirkpatrick, David. *The Facebook Effect: The Inside Story of the Company That Is Connecting the World.* New York, NY: Simon & Schuster, 2010.

Lüsted, Marcia Amidon. *Mark Zuckerberg: Facebook Creator* (Essential Lives). Edina, MN: ABDO Publishing Company, 2012.

Lüsted, Marcia Amidon. *Social Networking: MySpace, Facebook, & Twitter* (Technology Pioneers). Edina, MN: ABDO Publishing Company, 2011.

Parks, Peggy J. *Online Social Networking* (Compact Research). San Diego, CA: ReferencePoint Press, 2011.

Ryan, Peter K. *Social Networking* (Digital and Information Literacy). New York, NY: Rosen Central, 2011.

Woog, Adam. *Mark Zuckerberg, Facebook Creator* (Innovators). Detroit, MI: KidHaven Press, 2009.